HOW ANIMALS USE TOOLS

THE ANIMAL TOOLKIT

STEVE JENKINS & ROBIN PAGE

CLARION BOOKS
An Imprint of HarperCollins*Publishers*
Boston   New York

Humans use tools to help them work, play, eat, fight, and more. Animals also use tools, sometimes for the same reasons. Scientists who study animals don't always agree on just what a tool is. In this book, a tool is an object that an animal manipulates and uses to affect its environment, another animal, or itself. A twig used by a monkey to spear termites is a tool. But a tree trunk used by a bear to scratch its back is not.

A tool might be a rock or a stick. It could be a coconut shell or a leaf. A tool might even be another living creature.

Some animals, such as insects and fish, are born with the ability to be tool users. Others, such as birds and monkeys, figure out how to use tools by watching other animals. Read this book, and perhaps you'll learn new ways to crack an egg, sew a nest, or protect your tender nose.

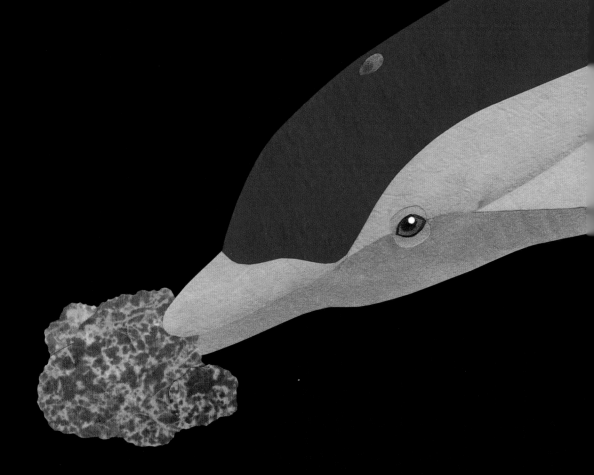

Drummer boy

Other than humans, the **palm cockatoo** is the only animal we know of that uses an object to make rhythmic sounds. A male bird selects a stick, shapes it with his beak, and uses it to tap out a beat on a tree limb. He's doing this to impress and attract a female cockatoo.

stick

palm cockatoo

shaping the drumstick

calling all females

Egg breaker

The **Egyptian vulture** has a taste for ostrich eggs. But there's a problem. The ostrich's eggshell is too tough for the vulture to break with its beak. So the vulture picks up a rock and throws it at the egg until it shatters.

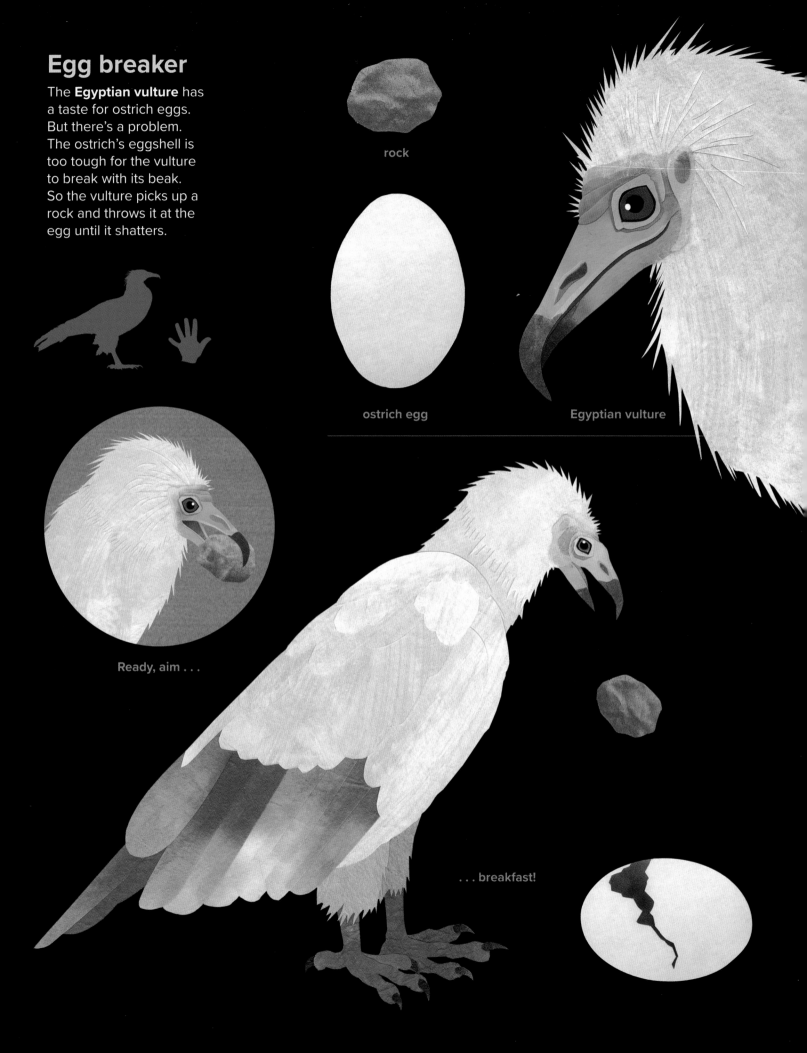

rock

ostrich egg

Egyptian vulture

Ready, aim . . .

. . . breakfast!

Eat, drink, fight

Like humans, **chimpanzees** use lots of different tools. A stick can be a spear or a termite-catching device. A handful of wadded-up leaves makes a sponge — handy for taking a drink. Chimpanzees throw stones, using them as a weapon. Males will also throw stones at a tree. We're not sure why they do this — it may be to make a loud noise that attracts a female or warns other males to stay away.

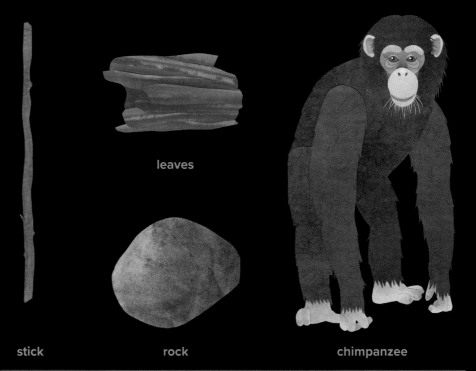

leaves

stick

rock

chimpanzee

fishing for termites

Throwing a rock at a tree makes a satisfying boom sound.

a spear

A leaf makes a handy sponge.

Don't forget to floss

Apes and monkeys use sticks, plant fibers, and even human hair (ouch!) to clean and floss their teeth.

stick and human hair

mandrill (a monkey)

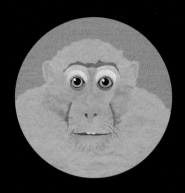

macaque (a monkey)

keeping that smile bright

This won't hurt — much.

time to floss

Many primates use tools. **Capuchins** and chimpanzees both use a stone to crack open nuts or shellfish.

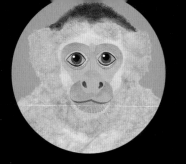

capuchin (a monkey)

chimpanzee (an ape)

stone

Watch your fingers!

crushing a nut

Baby's first meal

Before laying her egg, a female **thread-waisted wasp** digs a hole. Next, she paralyzes a caterpillar with her sting. She drags the helpless larva into the hole and lays a single egg on it. Finally, she fills in the hole, using a stone to pack down the soil that covers her nest. When the egg hatches, there will be a meal waiting for her hungry offspring.

thread–waisted wasp

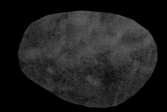

stone

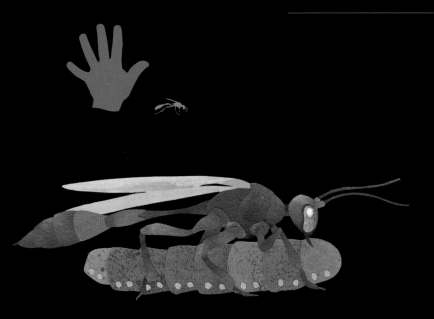

the unfortunate caterpillar

so glad you could come for dinner

securing the nest

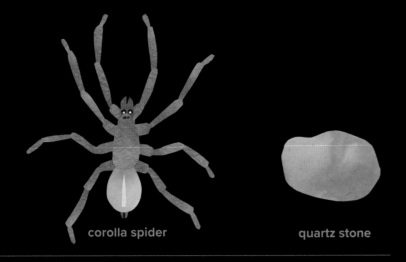

corolla spider

quartz stone

A trap of silk and stone

The **corolla spider** is also called the seven-stone spider. It collects quartz stones — usually seven of them — and arranges them around its burrow. (Quartz is especially good at transmitting vibrations.) The spider attaches a silk thread to each stone and touches the threads with her legs. When an insect brushes against one of the stones, it makes the silk threads vibrate. The spider feels the vibration, lunges, and grabs its prey.

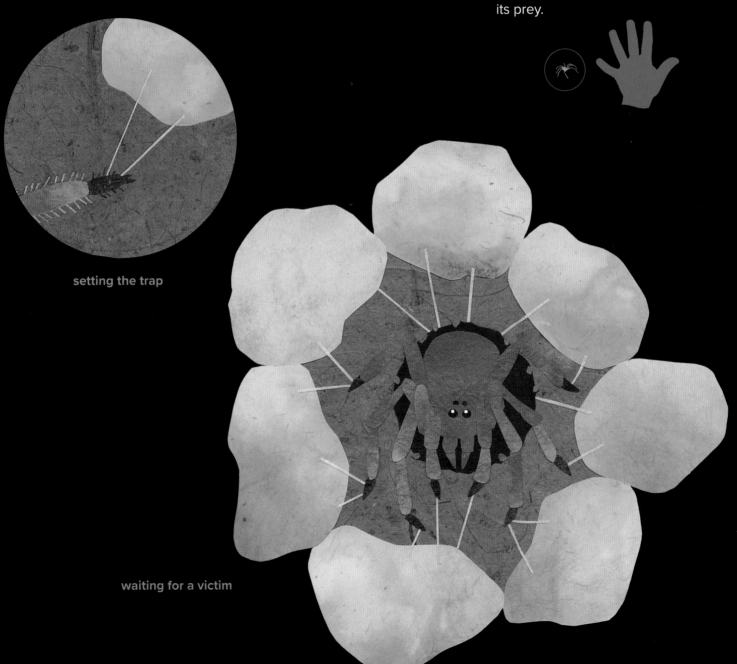

setting the trap

waiting for a victim

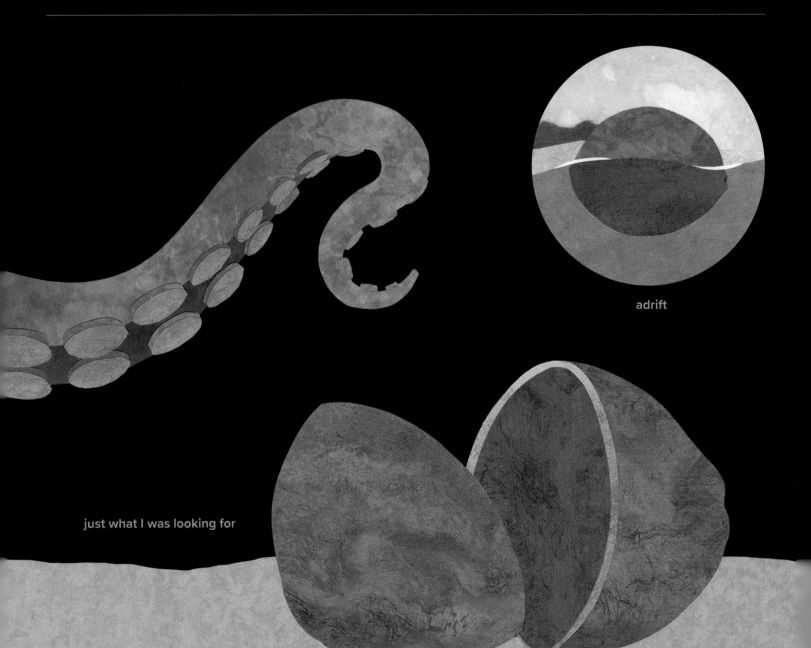

Mobile home

Sometimes a coconut falls into the sea, sinks to the seafloor, and breaks in two. If a **coconut octopus** finds the halves of a coconut shell . . .

coconut

coconut octopus

adrift

just what I was looking for

. . . it carries them along as a portable shelter. When danger threatens, the octopus tucks itself inside and pulls the halves of the shell together.

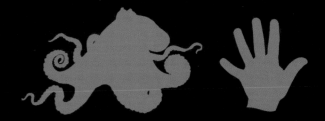

Watch me disappear.

Tough crab

The **boxer crab** defends itself with a pair of venomous sea anemones. It plucks them from the seafloor and displays them like boxing gloves. Fish, eels, and other predators want to avoid the anemones' stinging cells, so they try for easier prey.

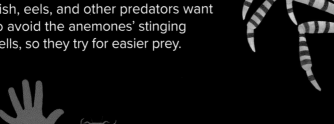

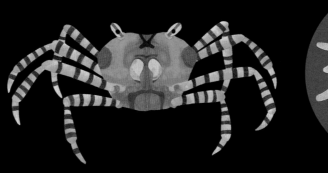

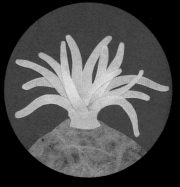

boxer crab

anemone

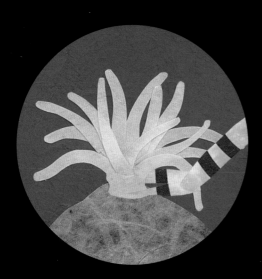

Choose your weapons.

This crab is ready to rumble.

Better back off!

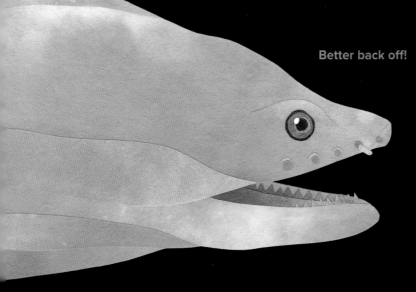

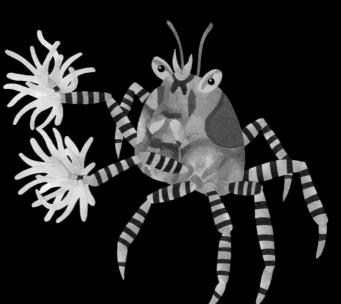

Seamstress

The female **common tailorbird** uses spiderweb silk or plant fibers as thread and her beak as a needle. She stitches the edges of a leaf together to make a nest, then pads it with grass, feathers, and other soft materials.

leaf

spiderweb silk

tailorbird

collecting thread

one last stitch

padding the nest

South American cichlid

leaf

Protective parents

The female **South American cichlid** lays her eggs on a leaf. She and her mate choose one that is large enough to hold her eggs but easy to pick up and carry. If danger threatens, the parents will move their precious cargo to a safer location.

This leaf is just right.

Let's get these eggs to safety.

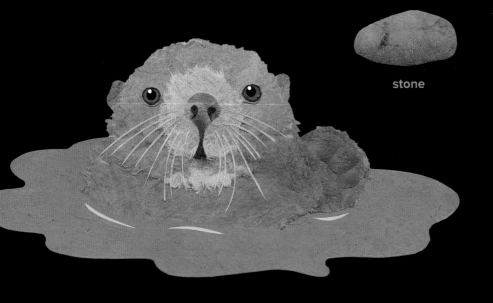

stone

Seafood

A **sea otter** picks up a stone from the seafloor and stores it in a pouch formed by a flap of skin under each arm. When the otter finds a clam or mussel, it floats on its back, places the stone on its chest, and smashes the shellfish against the stone to get to the tender morsel inside.

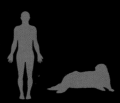

sea otter

looking for the perfect stone

time for a snack

Useful leaves

The **orangutan** uses leaves in creative ways. This gentle ape makes a kind of glove out of leaves. This protects its hand as it picks and handles spiky rainforest fruit. A large leaf also makes a good umbrella in a rainstorm.

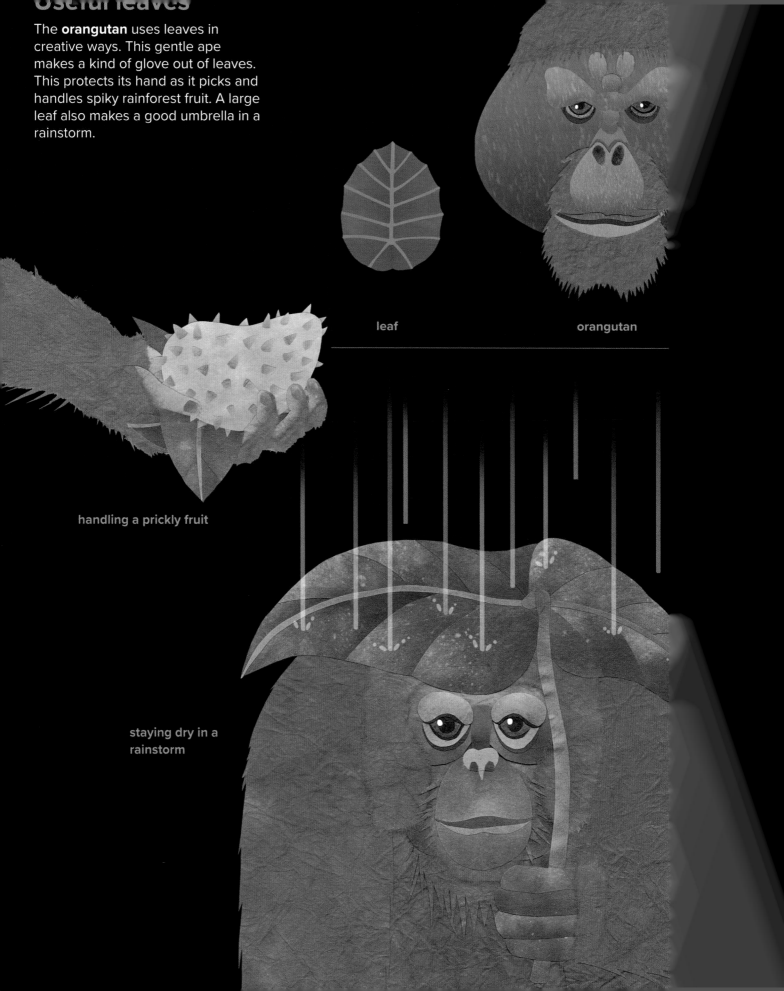

leaf

orangutan

handling a prickly fruit

staying dry in a rainstorm

A stick is a versatile tool. It can be used to probe a termite nest or separate the tasty seeds of the neesia fruit from the irritating fibers that surround them. Orangutans also use a stick to check the depth of a pond or stream.

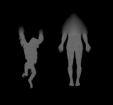

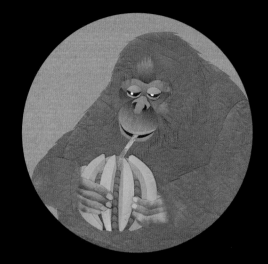

stick

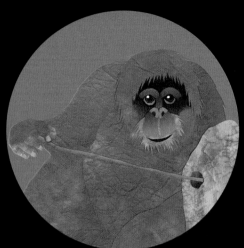

snagging termites

picking out the tasty seeds

How deep is this water?

Clever bird

The **crow** is one of the first animals that scientists recognized as a tool user. Since then, many examples of tool use by this intelligent bird have been found. Crows fashion a tool for spearing grubs by trimming a spiny-edged leaf. And young crows have pretend sword fights with sticks.

crow

trimmed leaf

stick

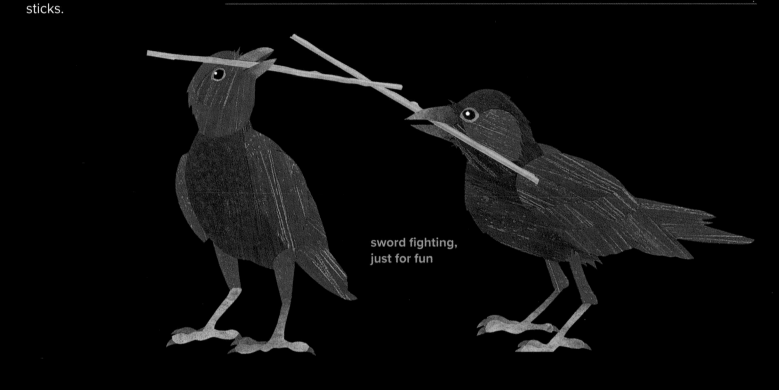

sword fighting, just for fun

impaling a grub

Spiny

The **woodpecker finch** plucks and trims a cactus spine. It uses the needle-like spine to extract insect larvae from tree trunks and branches.

cactus

woodpecker finch

Careful!

probing for insects

Hunting with fire

Birds known as fire raptors — such as this **black kite** — carry burning branches from a wildfire to an unburned spot. They start new fires to flush out the small animals they hunt.

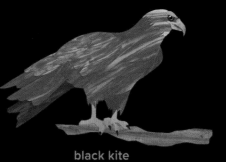

black kite

burning stick

fire starter

A quokka flees the flames . . .

flushing out its prey

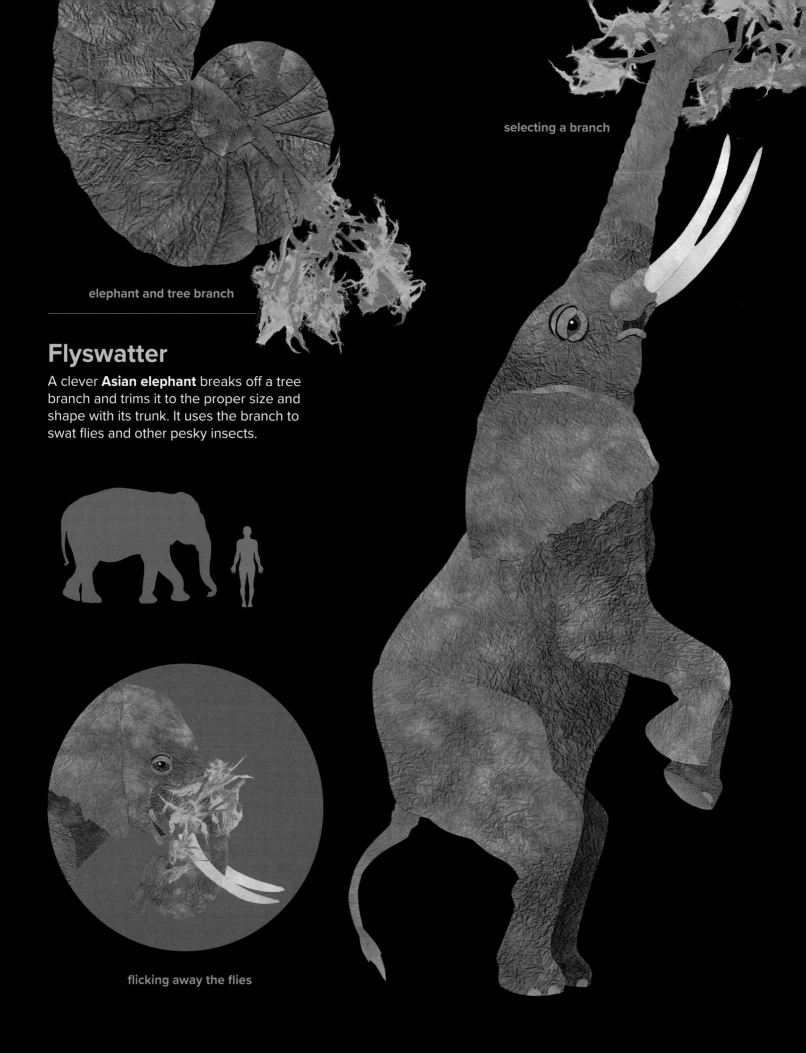

selecting a branch

elephant and tree branch

Flyswatter

A clever **Asian elephant** breaks off a tree branch and trims it to the proper size and shape with its trunk. It uses the branch to swat flies and other pesky insects.

flicking away the flies

Good riddance

Like many birds, **puffins** can be tormented by ticks. But the puffin takes matters into its own beak. It uses a stick to pry the parasites from its body. Puffins also use a stick just to scratch an itch.

puffin

stick

choosing a stick

tick

pest removal

Rock rubbing

Every spring, **grizzly bears** molt — they shed the dense layer of fur that kept them warm through the winter. A bear will scratch itself with its claws or rub its body against a tree to remove the old fur. And some bears use a tool — such as a rough, barnacle-covered rock — to speed up the process.

river rock

grizzly bear

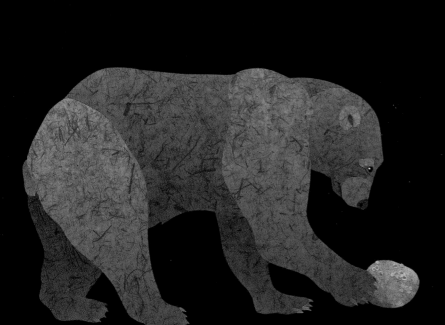

choosing a rock

The rock works best on wet fur.

That feels good!

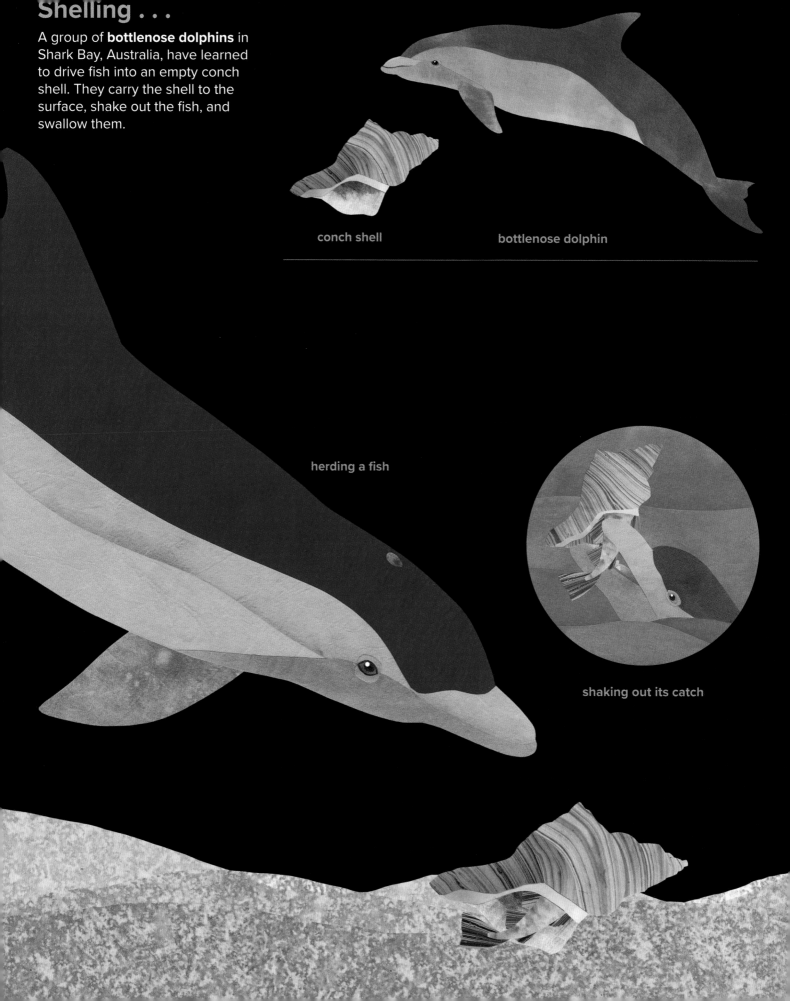

Shelling . . .

A group of **bottlenose dolphins** in Shark Bay, Australia, have learned to drive fish into an empty conch shell. They carry the shell to the surface, shake out the fish, and swallow them.

conch shell

bottlenose dolphin

herding a fish

shaking out its catch

. . . and sponging

The same kind of dolphin holds a
sponge in its mouth to protect its
tender beak as it probes the rocks
and coral of the seafloor. When the
dolphin flushes out a fish, it drops
the sponge and grabs its prey.

sponge

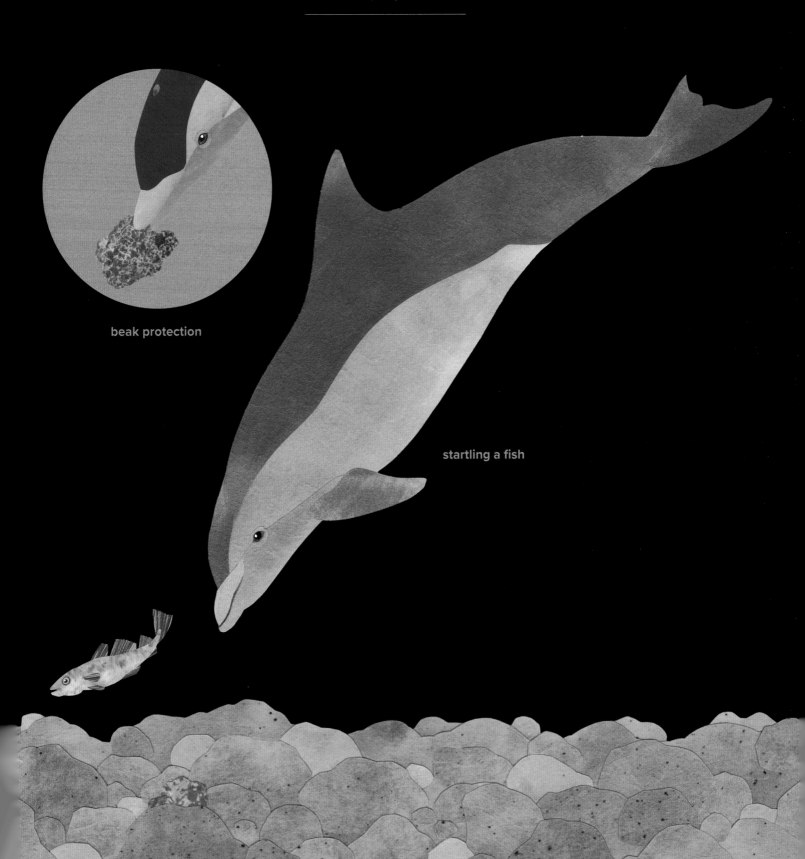

beak protection

startling a fish

Dig it

Digging a burrow in hard, rocky earth is a tough job. The **pocket gopher** uses a stone to help break up the soil.

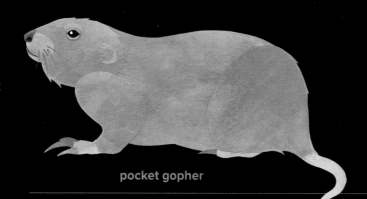

pocket gopher

stone

making a burrow

home sweet home

More information about the animals in this book

The **palm cockatoo** lives in the woodlands and rainforests of New Guinea and northern Australia. It feeds on fruit, seeds, and insects, and reaches two feet (61 centimeters) in length. The bird's colorful cheek patches change from red to yellow when it is excited. In one drumming session, a male cockatoo may strike a hollow tree or branch with its stick or hard seed pod as many as 200 times.

The **Egyptian vulture** feeds on carrion — dead animals — but also preys on live birds, reptiles, and small mammals. It eats the eggs of other birds, cracking open smaller ones with its beak. From beak to tail, this vulture is about two feet (61 centimeters) long. It is found in southern Europe, northern Africa, the Middle East, and Central Asia.

The **chimpanzee**, our closest animal relative, inhabits the forests and savannas of central Africa. A large male chimpanzee can weigh 150 pounds (68 kilograms) and stand almost five feet (1½ meters) tall. Females are smaller. This intelligent ape lives in groups of as many as 150 animals. It feeds on fruit, leaves, nuts, bark, roots, termites and other insects, birds' eggs, and small animals. Chimpanzees have been known to hunt monkeys using sticks as spears.

The **mandrill**, at three feet (91 centimeters) in length, is the world's largest monkey. It lives in the rainforests of central Africa in troops of up to 200 monkeys. The dominant males in the troop have the most intensely colored faces (they also have bright red-and-blue rear ends). The mandrill has a varied diet. It eats mostly plants, but also feeds on insects, scorpions, frogs, snakes, eggs, and small mammals. It has cheek pouches in which it can store food to be eaten later.

There are about two dozen species of **macaque**. These monkeys are found in rainforests, open woodlands, and urban environments in northern Africa and throughout much of Asia. They are up to two feet (61 centimeters) long, not including their tail. In the wild, they feed on plants, insects, mushrooms, and small animals. Macaques that live near humans can be a nuisance, stealing food, littering, and sometimes biting people.

Capuchins live in Central America and parts of South America. They inhabit open woods and rainforests, where they eat fruits, nuts, insects, shellfish, birds' eggs, and small animals. The capuchin's body is about 20 inches (51 centimeters) in length. It gets its name from its cap of dark hair, which reminded early European explorers of the hooded robes of a religious order of monks known as the Capuchin Friars.

Named for its extremely narrow waist, the **thread-waisted wasp** reaches two inches (5 centimeters) in length. The adult wasp drinks flower nectar and eats small insects. It stings and paralyzes caterpillars to feed to its larva. This insect is found throughout North America.

Including its legs, the **corolla spider** is about one-half inch (1¼ centimeters) across. It inhabits the Namib Desert in southern Africa, where the wind and drifting sand make building a web an ineffective way to trap its prey. Instead, the spider digs a burrow, lines it with silk, and surrounds it with stones. It waits in this burrow until an ant or other insect touches one of the stones surrounding its nest.

The warm, shallow waters of the western Pacific Ocean are home to the **coconut octopus**, also known as the veined octopus. Including its arms, it is about six inches (15 centimeters) long. It preys on crabs, shrimp, and clams. Small coconut octopuses will sometimes use a discarded clamshell — rather than a coconut — as a shelter.

The **boxer crab**, or pom-pom crab, lives in the ocean waters around Hawaii and the islands of the Indo-Pacific. It is a small crab, with a body measuring about one inch (2$\frac{1}{2}$ centimeters) across. Boxer crabs are omnivores. They eat plants, tiny animals, and carrion. This little crab displays a pair of anemones for defense because its claws are too small to protect it against predators. The anemones benefit from this arrangement by getting scraps of the crab's meals. If the boxer crab can find only one anemone, it will tear it into two pieces. Each piece will become a new anemone.

The **common tailorbird** lives in India and Southeast Asia. It is a small bird, about five inches (13 centimeters) long. Tailorbirds feed on insects,

fruit, and seeds. A female sews the nest together, then she and her mate collect soft plant fibers to fill it and take turns incubating the eggs and feeding the nestlings after they hatch.

The **South American cichlid** is found in the rivers of central South America. These fish are mouth brooders. Once the eggs hatch, the parents protect their offspring from predators by holding the little fish in their mouth. Adults are about 4$\frac{1}{2}$ inches (11$\frac{1}{2}$ centimeters) long. They eat aquatic plants and insects.

The thickest fur coat of any mammal keeps the **sea otter** warm as it hunts for shellfish, sea urchins, crabs, and fish in the cold waters of the northeastern Pacific Ocean. Sea otters, which reach four feet (122 centimeters) in length, were once hunted almost to extinction for their fur pelts. They are now protected and are gradually increasing in number. Without otters to keep their population under control, sea urchins would multiply and devour the kelp forests that are home to many other sea creatures. A group of sea otters floating in the ocean is called a raft.

The **orangutan** lives in the rainforests of Borneo and Sumatra — islands in the South Pacific. Though males can weigh as much as 200 pounds (91 kilograms) and stand more than four feet (1$\frac{1}{4}$ meters) tall, these apes spend most of their time in the treetops. They are gentle and intelligent, and feed on fruit, berries, nuts, bark, and insects. Dominant males develop flanges — disc-like cheeks that give them a round, flat face. Orangutans are critically endangered by illegal hunting and the loss of their habitat to human development.

Species of crows are found on every continent except South America and Antarctica. The species that has been most studied for its tool use is the **New Caledonian crow**, which inhabits an island in the South Pacific. This highly intelligent bird, which is about 16 inches (41 centimeters) long, uses leaves and sticks to probe for insect larvae. It also eats eggs, frogs, lizards, and small mammals.

The **woodpecker finch** is an inhabitant of the Galápagos Islands. Its diet consists of insects and insect larvae — especially wood-boring beetle larvae — as well as seeds and fruit. These birds are about six inches (15 centimeters) long. They have an unusually short tongue, which may explain why they developed the ability to use cactus spines and twigs to probe for their prey.

For centuries, native Australian people have reported that some birds of prey, or raptors, spread wildfires to frighten their prey into the open. Many scientists doubted this at first, but have since witnessed this behavior themselves. One of the birds that uses this hunting technique is the **black kite**. It is found throughout much of Europe, Asia, Africa, and Australia. It eats fish, small animals, and carrion. These birds are graceful in the air, with a wingspan of five feet (1¹/₂ meters).

Standing 10 feet (3 meters) tall and weighing as much as 11,000 pounds (4,990 kilograms), the **Asian elephant** is the world's second-largest land animal (only the African elephant is larger). It lives in India and Southeast Asia in small family groups led by an elder female. Elephants can eat 300 pounds (136 kilograms) of food a day, mostly grass, leaves, and plant stems. The elephant's trunk is impressive. It is strong enough to uproot a tree and delicate enough to handle an egg without breaking it.

Atlantic puffins nest on the seashores of the North Atlantic, where they dig burrows and line them with grass and feathers. They catch fish and small ocean animals by diving into the sea. Puffins are about 13 inches (33 centimeters) long. They may spend months or years at sea, returning to land to breed and raise a single chick.

The **grizzly bear** is a variety of brown bear that lives in North America. It is found in western Canada and in mountainous parts of the northwest United States. The polar bear and brown bear are the world's largest predators on land. Grizzly bears can reach 1,500 pounds (680 kilograms) in weight and stand ten feet (3 meters) tall, though most are smaller. They are omnivores, eating animals as large as elk and moose as well as squirrels, rabbits, frogs, insects, roots, berries, and other plant foods. Most grizzly bears live in cold habitats and spend the winter hibernating in a cave or den.

The **bottlenose dolphin** is one of the most intelligent animals. It is found in oceans worldwide, except for the polar regions. Dolphins are mammals, and must come to the surface regularly to breathe. The bottlenose dolphin reaches 13 feet (4 meters) in length. Fish are the main component of the dolphin's diet. It also eats squid, shrimp, and crabs. Some dolphins have learned to use tools by watching other dolphins.

The **pocket gopher** gets its name from its large, fur-lined cheek pouches. These pouches store food — roots, tubers, and aboveground plants that the gopher carries back to its burrow. The burrow, which is typically used by a single gopher, includes a network of underground tunnels and food-storage rooms. These rodents are about seven inches (18 centimeters) long. They are found throughout much of North America. Because they dig holes in lawns and gardens, many people consider gophers to be pests.

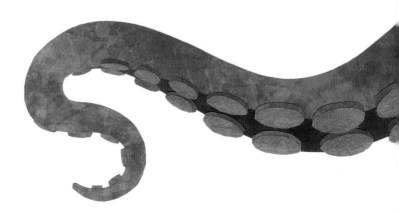

For Alec —S.J. & R.P.

Bibliography

Amazing Animal Tool-Users and Tool-Makers. By Leon Gray. Capstone Press, 2015.

Animal Architects. By James R. Gould and Carol Grant Gould. Basic Books, 2007.

Animal Tool Behavior: The Use and Manufacture of Tools by Animals. By Robert W. Shumaker, Kristina R. Walkup, and Benjamin B. Beck. Johns Hopkins University Press, 2011.

Chimps Use Tools and Other Amazing Facts about Apes and Monkeys (I Didn't Know That). By Claire Llewellyn. Millbrook Press, 1999.

Crafty Creatures and the Tools They Use. By Ellen Jackson. Charlesbridge, 2014.

Engineering Animals: How Life Works. By Mark Denny and Alan McFadzean. The Belknap Press, 2011.

Orangutan Hats and Other Tools Animals Use. By Richard Haynes and Stephanie Laberis. Candlewick, 2021.

Termites on a Stick. By Michele Coxon. Starbright Books, 2009.

Tool Use in Animals: Cognition and Ecology. By Crickette M. Sanz. Cambridge University Press, 2013.

Clarion Books is an imprint of HarperCollins Publishers.

Animal Toolkit
Text copyright © 2022 by Steve Jenkins and Robin Page
Illustrations copyright © 2022 by Steve Jenkins

clarionbooks.com

The illustrations are torn- and cut-paper collage.
The text was set in Proxima Nova.
Design by Steve Jenkins

ISBN: 978-0-358-24444-8

Manufactured in Italy
RTLO 10 9 8 7 6 5 4 3 2 1

First Edition